Young Hee Kim
Dae Young Kim

Network Architecture with Recursive Addressing

Young Hee Kim
Dae Young Kim

Network Architecture with Recursive Addressing

LAP LAMBERT Academic Publishing

Imprint

Any brand names and product names mentioned in this book are subject to trademark, brand or patent protection and are trademarks or registered trademarks of their respective holders. The use of brand names, product names, common names, trade names, product descriptions etc. even without a particular marking in this work is in no way to be construed to mean that such names may be regarded as unrestricted in respect of trademark and brand protection legislation and could thus be used by anyone.

Cover image: www.ingimage.com

Publisher:
LAP LAMBERT Academic Publishing
is a trademark of
International Book Market Service Ltd., member of OmniScriptum Publishing Group
17 Meldrum Street, Beau Bassin 71504, Mauritius
Printed at: see last page
ISBN: 978-620-3-41009-9

Network Architecture with

Recursive Addressing

Young Hee KIM & Dae Young KIM

Contents

Table of Figures

I. INTRODUCTION

Scalability of the Internet has long been recognized as one of its major problems. Explosion of DFZ (Default Free Zone) routing tables, one aspect of the problem, has resulted from Internet's inability of efficient multi-homing, for which semantic overloading of the IP address has been blamed [1]. This semantic overloading, that IP addresses are used as both IDentifiers (IDs) and Locators (Locs) for nodes, has also been perceived as against the naming and addressing principles [2] ~ [4] and so as the main obstacle hindering the Internet from providing seamless mobility and multihoming.

The argument was that a number of networking anomalies arise because the IP address which is primarily assigned to the node's interface (interface address) is also used as the node address for end-to-end transport connections. Since the interface address is coupled with the subnet identifier (ID) and so changes as a node moves across subnets, the transport connection would break at every such move of a node. Mobile nodes would suffer significantly from this frequent connection breakage unless an additional functionality like Mobile IP is incorporated. This semantic overloading (the interface address as 'where' and the node address as 'what') of the IP address was also recognized as the main reason for the Internet's incompetence in multihoming and so for the explosion of the default-free zone (DFZ) routing tables [1].

In the past 20 years, the idea of Loc/ID Separation (LIS) has been a hype in networking research and a considerable number of proposals have been introduced with varying success. LIS solutions are based on the view that separate networking objects representing each semantics (what and where) are indispensable necessities in networking architecture, and hence all offered solutions deal with two number spaces to accommodate the overloaded semantics. HIP [5] maintains the IP address intact loaded with its locator semantics and introduces separate host-identity for use in transport connections. ILNP [6] builds on global node IDs as identifiers and subnet (or equivalently link) prefixes as locators. LISP [7] relies on usual use (as both the node address and the interface address) of the semantically-overloaded global IP address (oddly called Endpoint ID or EID) within a site, while each site is again mapped to a global IP address called Routing Locator (RLOC). In effect, LISP constructs a two-tier nested addressing by naming nodes plus associated interfaces with global IP addresses and naming a collection of nodes (called LISP sites) with another global IP address.

This book discusses an architecture, named NARA, based on local addressing and a logical design drastically different from known LIS solutions in responding to the concern about the semantic overloading of the IP address. The generic architecture NARA is then projected on IPv6 as an implementation example. Instead of introducing a new number space to unload the equivocal semantics of the IP address, the specific implementation, called SID6 (Subnet ID Deprecated for IPv6), removes the interface semantics of the Global Unicast IPv6 address which is then to exclusively identify a node and so is to be used solely as the node address. The approach is based on the view that not both semantics are necessary in networking. That is, all that is needed is the node address, and the location information can be obtained indirectly through nodes' neighbor relations assisted by link-state routing protocols.

Following sections discuss the architectural rationale for this new paradigm, the architecture of NARA, and construction details of SID6 as a logical design for NARA thereof. Consequential advantages of this new paradigm are discussed before concluding the book.

II. ARCHITECTURAL RATIONALE

A. Links-First Model

Saltzer [4] states that there are four primary object types to be named in networking; services (users), nodes, attachment points (or points of attachment: PoAs), and paths (routes). Especially, an important message of his to our primary interest is that both nodes and PoAs should be named separately.

The way of thinking behind this notion might be the following:

1. Links are first-class citizens and so available before nodes come into play. Links provide PoAs (locators) as receptacles for nodes later to attach to.
2. Each node, already with an ID, attaches to one or more of these PoAs, thus further associating itself with one or more locators.

A transitional network graph in Step 1 where nodes are not yet at play may look like Fig. 1. Edges (lines) represent links and vertices (dots) the places reserved for nodes. Each PoA, i.e., each end of a link, is then named by a locator, ready for accepting a node.

Complete it may seem, this graph is incomplete for networking. With no routers in place to be specific, no packets can traverse the vertices. Unless vertices are filled with nodes, this is only a set of disconnected links, bearing no meaning from the perspective of networking. The links as yet are as good as nonexistent in strict view of networking.

Links will assume networking significance only when each vertex is filled (Step 2 above), like in Fig. 2, with either a relay node (router: R) or a leaf node (host: H). Note in the figure that each node, already given an ID, will additionally be associated with one or more locators. Thus, nodes are involved with two different types of names.

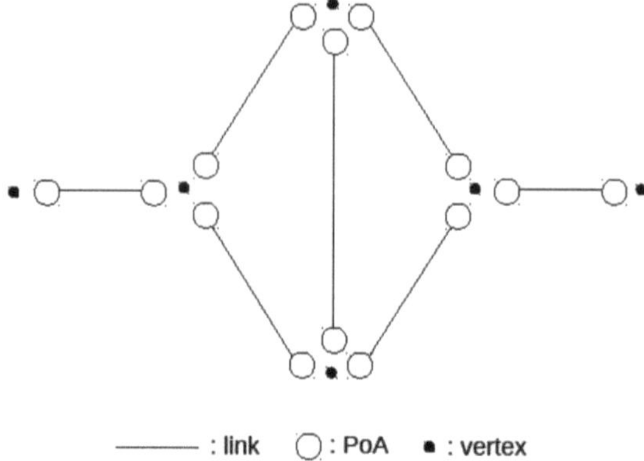

Fig. 1. Named links before nodes in place

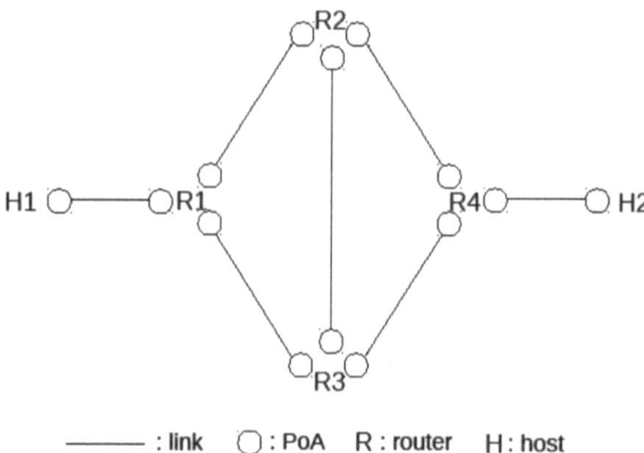

Fig. 2. Network graph with nodes in place

B. Nodes-First Model

One might ask oneself whether involving the two independent sets of names as in the previous subsection is absolutely necessary to accomplish seamless networking.

8

Fig. 3. Named nodes waiting to be connected

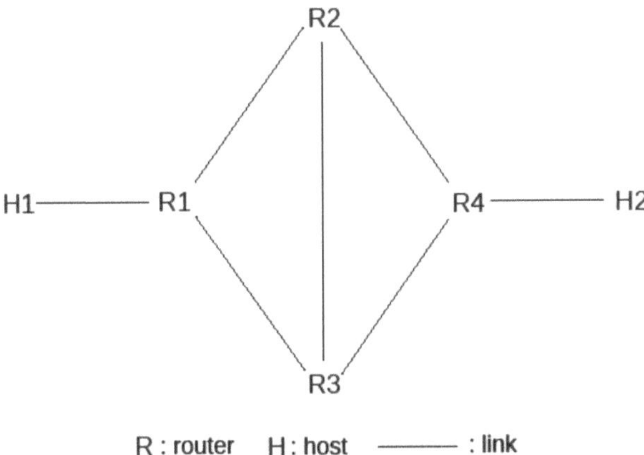

Fig. 4. Network graph with named nodes connected by unnamed links

Let us take another way of thinking in building a network:

1. There are nodes first, waiting to be connected. Nodes are named with node IDs.

2. As links are secured, nodes are connected by links. Links are not named.

3. With links connecting them, neighbor nodes establish connectivity relations.

4. Collection of all neighbor relations between nodes within a region of interest completes a network graph.

The steps in this way of thinking can be illustrated by Figs. 3 and 4. Fig. 3 shows named nodes in place waiting to be connected. As links are secured, the nodes are connected to form a network graph as in Fig. 4.

Note that reaching a complete network graph of Fig. 4 involves only one type of names, i.e., node IDs. Neighbor relations of the nodes are sufficient to build a network, and names of the links or PoAs are neither involved nor necessary. This is in stark contrast to the way a network is built through a different way of thinking associated with Figs. 1 and 2 in the previous subsection.

C. Fallacy of Duplicate Naming of Attachment Points

One might wonder why the second way of building a network above is possible. An explanation might be that naming PoAs (thus effectively naming links) is not a job of the network layer and so is not necessary; the very job belongs to the underlying link layer. That is, each PoA is already named in the underlying layer by a link-layer address; for example, by a MAC address. Naming PoAs again in the network layer is simply duplicate and redundant. By doing so, the same PoAs would be named twice, once by the link layer and again by the network layer [8].

It is to be reemphasized that this duplicate naming of PoAs in the network layer is unnecessary. Involving only one name type in the network layer is enough to build a network in the layer of interest. Not an additional separate name set but a set of neighbor relations between nodes completes a network.

III. NARA

This chapter proposes a network architecture, called NARA (Network Architecture with Recursive Addressing), based on recursive addressing with one name type. The Internet is modeled as a network of autonomous sites, each being a collection of nodes. Each site is named by a site address drawn from a global number space while each node is named by a node address drawn from a number space local to each site. Routing among sites depends solely on site addresses while that among nodes within each site on node addresses. Flat routing to render inherent mobility and cached routing as well as virtual routing to additionally cope with the table size are proposed. The model can recursively repeat itself both outwards and inwards in the network, enabling its applicability, for example, to inter-planetary as well as body area networks.

Node addresses in NARA are semantically overloaded. They are used for end-to-end connections as well as for routing. This is a stark contrast to prevalent arguments of LIS. Semantic overloading is not seen as an evil in NARA, but is rather positively exploited to provide inherent mobility and seamless multihoming.

Following sections describe the architecture of NARA and associated routing, along with implementation choices for a better chance of deployment.

A. Architecture

We describe NARA in a two-tier example. The same addressing and routing principles can be recursively repeated inwards and outwards off a given network tier. The outer (exterior) tier will be called the global network whereas a component of the inner (interior) tier will be a site. This two tier model closely resembles the Internet we know of (See Fig. 5).

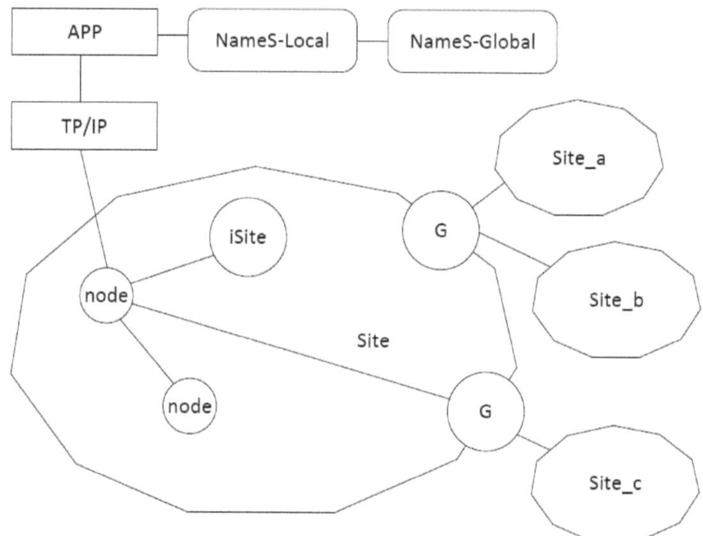

Fig. 5. Architectural overview of NARA

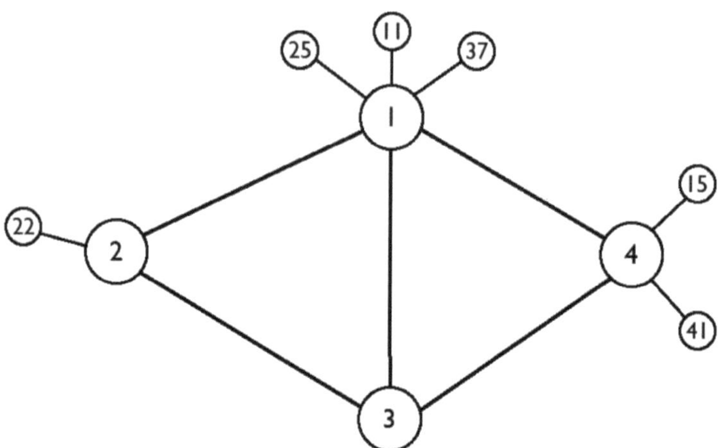

Fig. 6. Global network

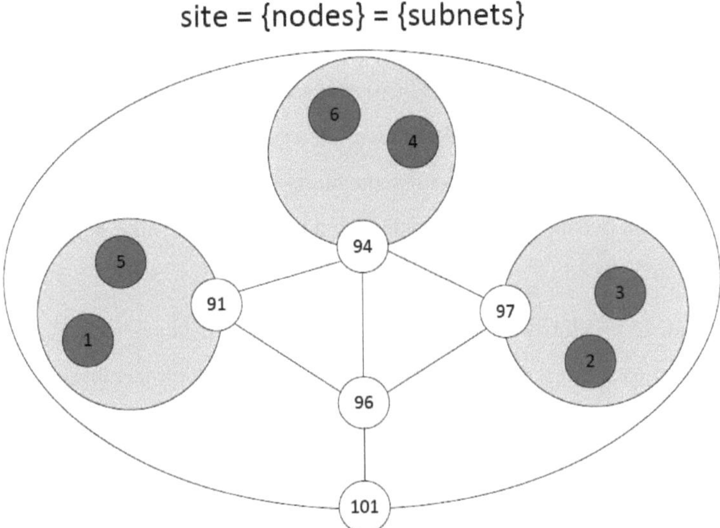

Fig. 7. Site, Node, Subnet

In a multi-tier network, the same architectural principles may be applied to any pair of adjacent tiers. In this respect, NARA can be considered as an instance of the recursive network architecture.

A1. Global network, Site, Node, Subnet

The global network is then a networked collection of sites (See Fig. 6). A site is an autonomous network with a collection of nodes. Nodes are either hosts (leaf nodes) or routers (relay nodes). A subset of hosts and an associated router forms a subnet. Therefore, a site can also be considered as a networked collection of subnets (See Fig. 7).

A2. Address

A full address of an entity in the lowest tier of an N-tier network is a tuple of {addr-1, addr-2, ..., adds-N}, where each 'addr-i' is called a partial address. In the two-tier example, the full address of a node reduces to a tuple of a pair of partial addresses, {node address, site address}. In our subsequent discussion, an 'address' stands for a full address whereas a partial address would carry a pre-descriptor like with node address, site address, etc.

Sites are named by global site addresses whereas nodes (hosts or routers) are by node addresses local to a given site. Each subnet is associated with a router and so can be identified by the router address. Therefore, the subnet address and the router address stand for the same and so can be used interchangeably.

Neither node- nor site-addresses bear topological significance; they each consume separate flat number spaces. Node addresses don't change while nodes are moving around within a site. Site addresses also don't change at migration between upstream network providers as well as at multihoming.

When routing scalability should be at risk, flat addresses might be replaced with virtual addresses which are aggregatable.

A3. Name

Each node is associated with a name, a character string. Names are global, i.e., are Fully Qualified Domain Name (FQDN)s. Since a node is associated with a name as well as with an address, there's one-to-one correspondence between a name and an address.

A4. Name Server

The FQDN of a node would be resolved first to a site address by an exterior (global) name server. A local name server then resolves the rest of the name to a local node address. Each part of the name will be resolved stepwise to an address valid in the relevant tier of the whole recursive network.

A5. Gateway

A site is bordered by at least one gateway router, as G in Fig. 5. In the case of multihoming, there'd be multiple gateways bordering a given site.

One of the important functions of the gateway is to change addresses of packets at border crossing. At exiting a site, the packet addresses (source and destination addresses in the header of a packet) would be changed from node addresses to site addresses. At entering a site, on the other hand, the change would be in the reverse direction, i.e., from site addresses to node addresses.

A6. Routing

If the site address is local, packets are delivered to an interior node. If it is foreign, packets are delivered to one of gateways.

Gateways participate in both interior and exterior routing. Interior routing is done on node addresses while exterior routing on site addresses. Node addresses are never exposed to exterior routing. That is, interior and exterior routings are orthogonal to each other.

A7. Transport Connection

Transport connections are involved with full (node-and site-) addresses. This is in contrast to routing wherein only partial (node- or site-) addresses are involved.

A8. Mobility

The address of a node doesn't change in moving around within a site. Hence, interior mobility is provided as an inherent feature of the architecture.

The address of a site doesn't change at migration from one provider to another. Hence, exterior mobility is provided also as an inherent feature of the architecture.

Inherent mobility breaks when aggregatable virtual addresses are employed instead of flat addresses.

A9. Recursion

Symmetry of network architecture repeats itself at each tier. The same generic architecture recurses inwards and outwards.

A node in a given site can itself be a site. That is, the node can be marked by a gateway and contain children nodes inside.

A site in the exterior tier corresponds to a node in the interior tier. The same architectural compositions and associated operations hold true in the exterior as within the site. Each transit site effectively reduces to a relay node (router) whereas each leaf site to a leaf node (host).

B. Interior Routing

There are two methods of interior routing of NARA. One is "Flat Routing" which operates when the network size is appropriate. The other is "Cached Routing" which operates when the size of the nodes in the site grows and the network operations are overwhelmed by the expansion of the routing table.

B1. Flat Routing

Packets interior to a site are routed solely on node addresses. Site addresses don't come into play in interior routing. Any link-state protocols can be applied to interior routing. Each router maintains a table of address tuples {(target) node, owner (subnet), next-hop (router)}. Tables are updated through routing information exchange between routers (See Fig. 8. Numbers associated with links are link costs).

Hosts may not involve themselves directly with such routing tables. It is up to routers to route packets exiting nodes. When a host moves from one subnet to another, such a membership change is immediately broadcast to all other routers in the site by the previous and/or newly-visited subnet router(s). Host mobility is thus inherent in interior routing and so is fast.

When a subnet moves along with the associated router, such a move will be perceived as a topological change of the network and will be immediately reflected in the routing tables through triggered link-state updates. Henceforth, (subnet) network mobility is also provided as an inherent feature of the routing (See Fig. 9).

Link-state updates are both periodic and event-driven or triggered. While periodic updates are a normal process, triggered updates help the routing system instantly reflect dynamic changes of the network state.

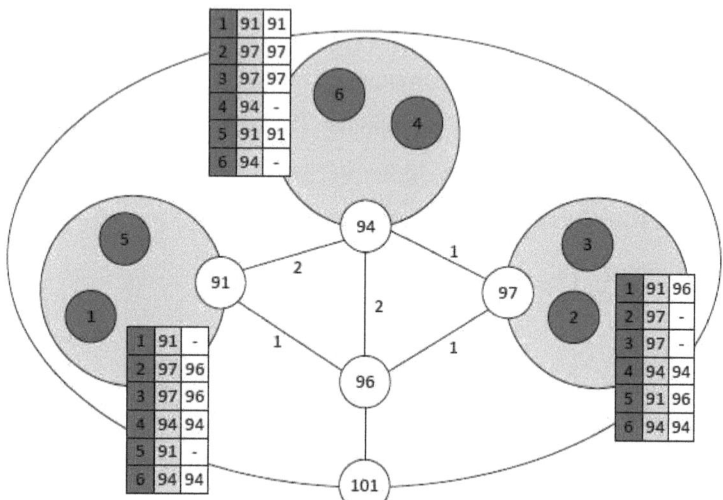

Fig. 8. Interior Flat Routing

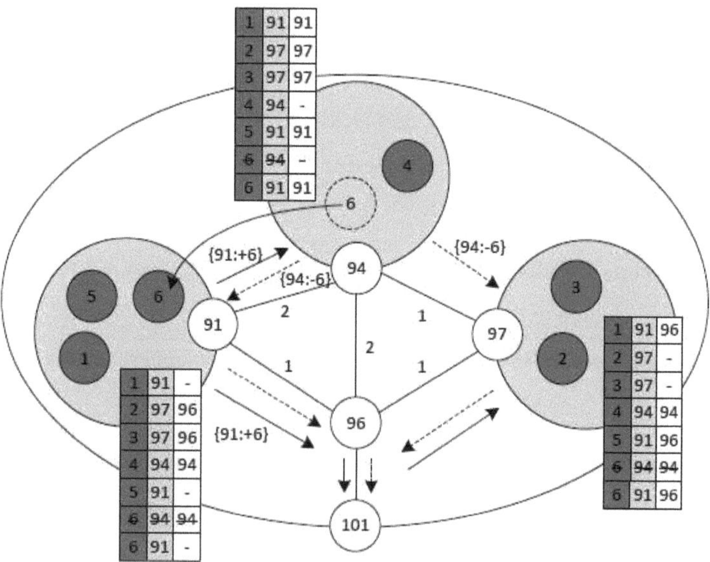

Fig. 9. Mobility in Interior Flat Routing

18

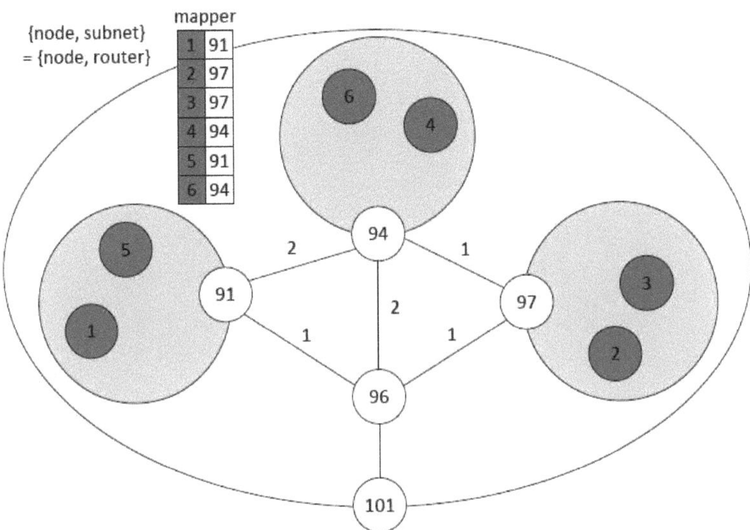

Fig. 10. Interior Cached Routing

With triggered updates, there might be a risk of broadcast storm in an environment of a very large number of agile nodes. Engineered tailoring shall reduce the risk to an affordable level.

B2. Cashed Routing

With flat routing, the size of the router table may grow with the number of nodes populated in a given site. As the site grows, the table size could become an operational burden. In this case, cached routing can be incorporated to compensate for the disadvantages of flat routing. Here, the routers would maintain tuples {host, owner, next-hop} only for active flows whereas the full population information {host, owner} would be stored in a separate population server (See Fig. 10).

19

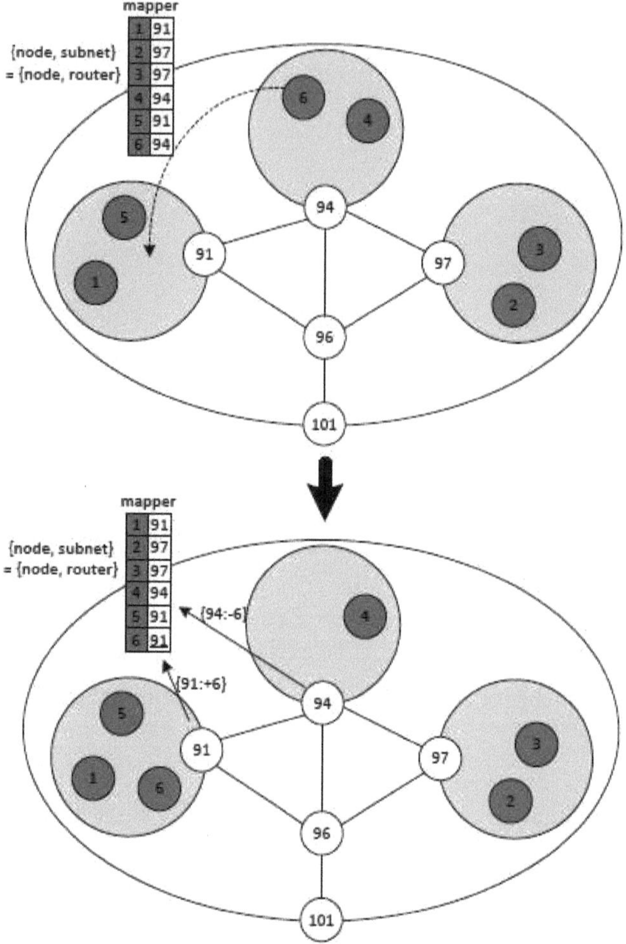

Fig. 11. Mobility in Interior Cached Routing

Processing of information for hosts and routers are different in this cached routing. Moving of a host is not broadcast to all routers but is notified only to the population server (mapper) which maintains an address table of {host, owner} tuples (See Fig. 11).

When the target host address of an incoming packet is missing in its routing cache, the router consults the population server to acquire the subnet address containing the target host address. The router then adds the entry of {host, owner, next hop} in its routing cache.

An entry in the cache for a specific host would be maintained only while the corresponding flow is judged to be active. As soon as the flow is deemed to be inactive, the entry in the cache would be purged.

As for the routers, they are involved in link-state routing in the background as usual. Moving of a subnet would trigger a link-state update, and hence the (subnet) network mobility would be provided seamlessly as with flat routing.

Cached routing as described here for interior routing can also be applied in the same way to exterior routing.

B3. Multiple Owners

Suppose one subnet is owned by multiple routers. Although rare, this may not be improbable. In this case, the subnet is identified by multiple router addresses, and is reachable through any of the associated routers.

C. Exterior Routing

Packets in the global tier, exterior to sites, are routed solely on site addresses. Node addresses are not advertised into the global tier.

Each transit sites can be considered to correspond, in a generic network graph, to relay nodes (routers) whereas leaf sites to leaf nodes (hosts). Therefore, symmetry of network architecture repeats itself at each tier.

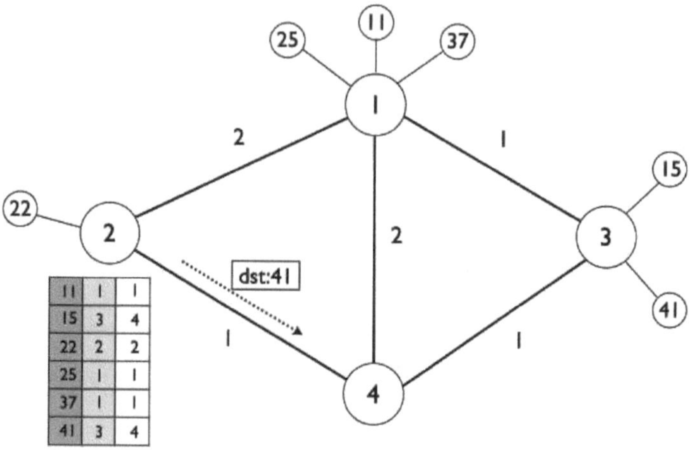

Fig. 12. Exterior Flat Routing

C1. Exterior Flat Routing

In a scenario of flat routing, site addresses are directly used in routing and forwarding decisions. Each transit gateway maintains a table of {(target) site, owner (transit site), next-hop (transit site)} address tuples. Tables are updated through routing information exchange between transit gateways. For multihomed target sites, multiple entries for the same target-site may exist with different owner site addresses.

Leaf gateways may not involve themselves directly with such routing tables. It is up to transit gateways to route packets exiting leaf sites (See Fig. 12).

C2. Virtual Routing

In a scenario of virtual routing, aggregatable addresses are used in order to shrink the routing table size. Transit gateways may use PA (Provider-Aggregatable) prefixes

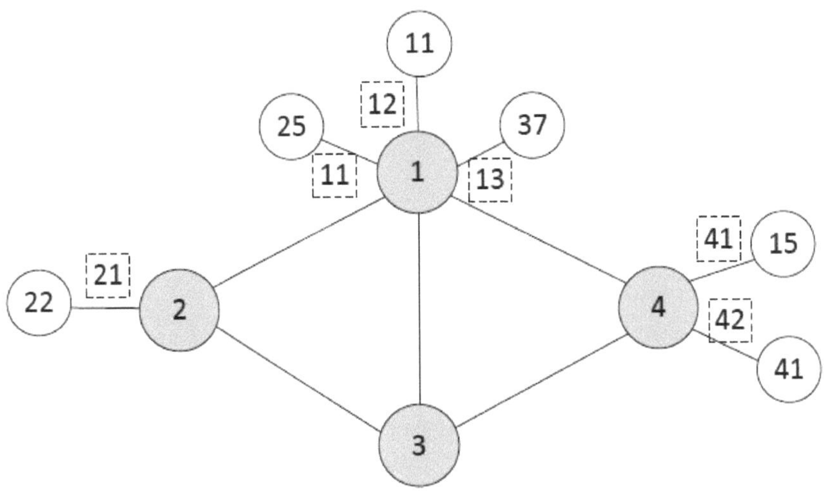

Fig. 13. Exterior Virtual Routing

as virtual addresses for routing instead of site addresses. Each site will then be associated with one or more (for multihoming) PA prefixes, with such mapping maintained by a mapping server in the global tier. A site address will be converted by an upstream transit gateway to a PA prefix at entering that upstream provider, and the PA prefix will subsequently be converted back to the site address at leaving the upstream provider into the downstream target site.

Leaf gateways themselves need not be aware of existence of such PA prefixes. They will continue to involve themselves only with site addresses, for source and target, and hence behave themselves the same way as they do with flat routing (See Fig. 13).

Virtual routing as described here for exterior routing can also be applied in the same way to interior routing.

D. Implementation Choices

Although the proposed network architecture of NARA is described in a generic way, it can be tailored for smooth and incremental deployment in the existing Internet.

D1. Site versus Domain

The description of a site in NARA closely resembles that of an Internet routing domain or Autonomous System (AS). As far as fast mobility is concerned, it better matches a routing area within a domain, in fact. For the sake of simplicity, we'd assume a single-area domain.

D2. Node Address

In principle, both IPv4 and IPv6 addresses can be used for local node addresses. Since 32 bits might be more than enough for most sites, use of IPv4 addresses might sometimes be more appealing. Use of IPv4 addresses ensures minimal changes to still existing vast population of IPv4 hosts. However, use of IPv6 address should be recommended wherever possible.

Node addresses are local; they are allocated by a corresponding local authority. Global uniqueness is not a requirement. It is to be noted that IP addresses adopted as such do not name interfaces anymore but do nodes themselves. That is, although IP addresses will continue to be used, their semantic interpretation will be changed.

D3. Site Address

In the case of IPv4 implementation, 32-bit IP addresses can be used for site addresses. 32 bits are long enough to accommodate a considerable number of sites that may additionally come into being in the global Internet. The uniqueness of the site addresses will be maintained by a global authority like IANA.

The routing prefix of a whole domain, i.e., the aggregate address of the whole PA addresses already assigned to a given domain, can be used as the site address if virtual routing is adopted.

One might wonder where to carry site addresses in the case of IPv4 addressing. It is proposed to carry them in the IPv4 option field of length 32 bits. Another option is to follow the scheme proposed in hIPv4 [9]. That is, node addresses and site addresses can be swapped by gateways (called Locator Swap Router in hIPv4) at exiting and entering given sites.

However, use of IPv6 address should be recommended wherever possible.

D4. Address Changes at Gateways

In addition to the use of the option field or swapping as described in the previous subsection, there might be even other ways of address change at gateways.

One such other way might be encapsulation/de-capsulation. That is, a packet leaving a site would be encapsulated into an outer packet header carrying the (source- and destination-) site addresses. In entering a site, on the other hand, the packet would be decapsulated to expose the in-site packet header carrying the node addresses instead.

Another way might be use of NAT (Network Address/Port Translator) at gateways. A node address/port pair would be translated to a site address for packets leaving a site, and vice versa. A rationale for this approach might be the current ubiquitous massive use of NATs throughout the whole Internet. The phenomena prevails so deeply in the current Internet infrastructure as to argue that it's time to consider middle-box communication as one of paradigms in reality.

A more elegant method might be concatenation of multi-tier addresses in the packet header in a fashion similar to the IPv6 Source Routing Extension Header. In entering a tier, the relevant address in the address list would be looked up for routing.

Independently of which implementation method should be used, change of packet addresses at crossing tier boundaries would cause some level of processing overhead to gateways, implying performance degradation. Also, security vulnerability might be of concern. However, observing the current field practice of the Internet operation wherein substantial middle boxes reside at gateways, in the form of firewalls and/or NATs, are widely employed, the negative impact on performance and security would be within a manageable nature.

D5. Name Server

In the two-tier model described here, names are globally unique. DNS can continue to be used with an extension; return {node address, site address} pairs instead of {IP address}.

The scope of names can be an issue in recursive repetition of this network architecture. If the tiers would recurse without bound inwards and/or outwards, demanding uniqueness of names in the entire resultant network may not be feasible because of excessive length of the names.

Name resolution may be done recursively. For example, if a remote node wants to get a body temperature of a human node, an application message "get body temperature" may first be targeted to the human node of an address pair {node, site}, for which a name server as in Fig. 10 has done the mapping. Then, the content of the message may be used to consult another name server encompassing the tier pair one level deeper, that is, the tier where the human body belongs and another covering the nodes inside the human body. This name server can then return an address pair {in-human node, human node} to continue address swapping to reach the final thermometer. That is to say, context-awareness may ensure recursive name service.

D6. Routing Protocols

OSPF or ISIS can be used for interior routing. A difference is that IP addresses (as node addresses) now point to nodes instead of interfaces. Changes to OSPF coding should be minimal. ISIS might be better suited in this sense because it inherently deals with node addresses.

Although other protocols, in principle, could also be used for exterior routing, BGP4 with some modification with virtual routing might be a choice more acceptable, as a start, to most existing ISPs and large transit sites.

IV. SID6

This chapter details how to construct the new architecture of NARA through novel choice of operational policies in various IPv6 protocols and some trivial modifications. Especially, inherent provision of intra-domain node- as well as subnet-mobility by use of the standard link-state intra-domain routing protocols is discussed.

This approach is drastically different from the known LIS solutions in responding to the concern about the semantic overloading of the IP address. Instead of introducing a new number space to unload the equivocal semantics of the IP address, the proposed approach, called SID6 (Subnet ID Deprecated for IPv6), removes the interface semantics of the Global Unicast IPv6 address which is then to exclusively identify a node and so is to be used solely as the node address.

The approach is based on the view that not both semantics are necessary in networking. That is, all that is needed is the node address, and the location information can be obtained indirectly through nodes' neighbor relations assisted by link-state routing protocols.

One major measure taken in SID6 for the purpose is to deprecate the subnet ID in the IP address. That is, the value of the ID is set to zero for all subnets within a routing domain. This ensures that the node address be kept invariant and thus transport connections don't break when nodes move across links (or subnets) within a domain.

Construction of SID6 is based on the existing legacy IPv6 network with minimal changes. In fact, the only significant change is to deprecate the subnet ID. The rest of the changes are minimal to null, and extensive discussions would highlight how the current system works intact with these changes. For the sake of our discussion, it is to be noted that site, (routing) domain, and Autonomous System (AS) are used interchangeably in this work. Also, although care should be taken to differentiate subtle semantic difference between the two, subnet and link will be used interchangeably.

A. IPv6 Address

The IPv6 address type of interest is the Global Unicast address which contains the subnet ID [10]:

```
IPv6 Global Unicast address
    = (interface address)
    = (subnet prefix, interface ID)
    = (global routing prefix, subnet ID, interface ID)
```

The interface ID is 64 bits long [10] while, according to IAB/IESG recommendations, the subnet ID is 16 bits long [11, 12].

Now, we reset the subnet ID, and the IPv6 Global Unicast address will no longer depend on the subnet ID; it doesn't change as a node moves across subnets within a domain:

```
IPv6 Global Unicast address
    = (global routing prefix, 0x0000, interface ID)
```

In order to keep the global uniqueness of the address, the interface ID should be unique within a domain. That is, the scope of the interface ID is the domain of interest in contrast to its usual scope of a subnet [10]. Duplicate Address Detection (DAD) would be affected through this new constraint. See Sec. IV-C for more discussion.

For the sake of SID6 description, we take the interface ID as the node ID. When a node has multiple interfaces, there would be multiple interface IDs associated. In that case, we pick the interface ID of the smallest value and take it as the node ID. The result is:

```
IPv6 Global Unicast address
    = (node address)
    = (subnet prefix, node ID)
    = (global routing prefix, 0x0000, node ID)
```

The node ID is unique for the node and invariant within a site or routing domain. The address is now a node address, not an interface address.

When a site is multi-homed on multiple Internet Service Providers (ISPs), it would be associated with multiple global routing prefixes and hence every intra-site node would be associated with multiple addresses. For seamless site-multihoming of such an instance, nodes should be able to receive inbound packets destined to any of such multiple addresses, and also be able to source outbound packets with one of such multiple addresses as appropriate.

Remember all we did here is to reset the subnet ID. And that, this is not any change in the definition of the IPv6 address format, but is just an operational choice. All others are natural corollary consequences with no enforcement of any significant artificial policies; the mechanism remains the same. We will subsequently see how other parts of the IPv6 networking continue to work correctly as usual with either some changes or no further substantial manipulation.

B. Neighbor Discovery

Addresses involved in ICMPv6-derived [13] messages of Neighbor Discovery (ND) for IPv6 [14] are either All-Nodes multicast addresses (FF02:0:0:0:0:0:0:1) or All-Routers multicast addresses (FF02:0:0:0:0:0:0:2), and both are agnostic to the subnet ID. Otherwise, the involved addresses are unicast or anycast addresses not anymore dependent on the subnet ID as prescribed in SID6.

As defined above, the subnet prefixes (global routing prefix + 0x0000) advertised by all routers within a domain are the same. Although substantially simplifying router configuration in regard to prefix loading, this necessitates the change in on-link determination. The original ND [14] specifies that a node considers an address to be on-link (reachable on the same link) if:

1. it is covered by one of the link's prefixes (e.g., as indicated by the on-link flag in the Prefix Information option), or
2. a neighboring router specifies the address as the target of a Redirect message.
3. a (solicited) Neighbor Advertisement message is received for the (target) address, or
4. any ND message is received from the address.

The latter two, however, have been deprecated by [15].

Criterion 2 should continue to be valid in SID6. However, Criterion 1 is of no more use since all prefixes are the same and hence the on-link flag loses its semantics. To be exact, the subnet prefix is not just link-local but rather site-local. Since on-link information cannot be obtained through prefixes provided by a pair procedure of Router Solicitation (RS) and Router Advertisement (RA), some other means has to be secured for on-link determination. For this purpose, we propose to add the following procedure to the ND protocol:

- When a node is first injected into a domain and attaches to a link, it might acquire prefix information through a pair of RS and RA, and auto-configure itself with a node address sanitary-checked through Duplicate Address Detection (DAD) described in the following subsection. It then multicasts an unsolicited Neighbor Advertisement (NA) to the link-local All-Nodes address, FF02:0:0:0:0:0:0:1, to explicitly notify all other nodes on the same link of its emergence. The source address of this NA shall be the node address of the new node, and the link-layer address shall also be included in an option. In addition, a new option shall be incorporated to indicate that every recipient of this unsolicited NA should return a unicast Neighbor Solicitation (NS) back to the sender. Since NA transmission is unreliable, it can be repeated MAX_NEIGHBOR _ADVERTISEMENT [14] times. The first NA should be issued after a random delay between 0 and MAX_RTR_SOLICITATION_DELAY [14] to avoid race condition among multiple newly emerging nodes.

- On receipt of this unsolicited NA, other nodes on the link should return a unicast NS back to the new node. In this action, issuing of each NS should be random delayed to avoid race condition. Also, the link-layer address of the responding node shall be included in each NS. Duplicate NAs received through retransmission shall be silently ignored.

- Successful receipt of such a returning NS determines the forward reachability from the new node's perspective; the responding address is on-link. The new node creates an entry for the responding address in Neighbor Cache. This is done for each responding address.

- For each of such returning NSs, the new node unicasts an NA to the responding address. Successful receipt of this NA by each responding node determines reachability from the responding node's perspective; the address of the new node is on-link. The responding node then creates an entry for the new node's address in its own Neighbor Cache.

- All addresses in Neighbor Cache of a node are considered to be on-link.

This new procedure differs from the existing ND procedure in that on-link determination is made not through Prefix List (for addresses with on-link flag set) but through Neighbor Cache. The role of Prefix List reduces simply to providing the global routing prefix(es) for the given site. Another difference is in regard to the semantics of the source address for NA and NS; whereas it is the sender's interface address in the original ND, it is the node address in SID6.

With the introduction of this revised procedure for on-link determination, it follows that Criterion 3 of the original on-link determination should be revived:

- When a solicited NA message is received for the target address, the address is confirmed to be on-link.

Criterion 4 remains deprecated.

C. Duplicate Address Detection

DAD per IPv6 Stateless Address Auto-configuration (SLAAC) is done for all unicast addresses by use of a pair of link-local ND messages, namely, NS and NA [16]. In SID6, however, DAD should be done site-wide, and hence new site-local messages should be introduced to do the job.

We name the new pair of ICMPv6 messages as Duplicate Solicitation (DS) and Duplicate Advertisement (DA). Also, we introduce a new type of multicast address named site-local Solicited-Node address defined in a way similar to the (link-local) Solicited-Node multicast address [10]:

```
Site-Local Solicited-Node Address: FF05:0:0:0:0:1:FFXX:XXXX
```

A site-local Solicited-Node address is formed by taking the low-order 24 bits of an address (unicast or anycast) and appending those bits to the prefix `FF05:0:0:0:0:1:FF00::/104` resulting in a multicast address in the range

```
FF05:0:0:0:0:1:FF00:0000 ~ FF05:0:0:0:0:1:FFFF:FFFF
```

A DS is multicast to a site-local Solicited-Node address formed with the unicast or anycast address of the target node. If the target address of the returning DA is tentative [16], it is an indication that the address is a duplicate. Both nodes should then refresh their addresses and repeat DAD until no duplicates are observed. An address is considered site-unique if none of the tests equivalent to the ones in Sec. 5.4 of SLAAC indicate the presence of a duplicate address within `RetransTimer` milliseconds after having sent `DupAddrDetectTransmits` DSs [16]. A side effect of this site-wide DAD is that uniqueness of the node ID(s) is confirmed site-wide.

D. Interior Gateway Protocols

A link-state Interior Gateway Protocols (IGP) is to be used in SID6; OSPFv3 [17] or IS-IS for IPv6 [18, 19]. The most important impact of SID6 on these link-state routing protocols is the way routers locate the hosts; they are not anymore locatable by link prefixes.

In SID6 operation of OSPFv3, host routes (full IPv6 node addresses) are to be included in intra-area-prefix-LSAs. For each of these host routes, the `PrefixOptions` `LA-bit` should be set and the `PrefixLength` should be set to 128 (host `PrefixLength`); see Section 4.4.3.9 of [17]. In SID6 operation of IS-IS for IPv6, host routes are to be included in the IPv6 Reachability entries, and will be handled in the same manner as other IPv6 Reachability entries [18, 19].

E. Other Address-Related Protocols

DHCPv6 [20] is not affected since most addresses involved there are link-local. The site-local All_DHCP_Servers multicast address in the case of Relay Agent is also intact for correct operation.

Default Address Selection [21] is not affected, either. One thing to note is in regard to scope comparison in selecting a source address for a multicast destination address; see Section 3.1 of [21]. The scope of the node address as defined in SID6 is global as well as site. Hence, the same source node address would be selected for a multicast destination address of site scope as well as of global scope as appropriate.

No other IPv6-address related protocols are affected, to the best knowledge of the authors.

V. CONSEQUENCES AND BENEFITS

In this chapter, we discuss the consequences and benefits of NARA in view of its IPv6 implementation SID6.

A. No Locator/ID Separation

SID6 does not introduce a separate number space extra to that already existing IPv6 address space; no locator/ID separation is pursued. Within a site, the node ID identifies a node whose location is done through an intra-domain link-state routing protocol. Between sites, the global routing prefix both identifies and locates a site. In fact, SID6 is an instance of recursive addressing as explored in NARA.

B. Inherent Intra-Domain Mobility

The most important consequence of SID6 is that the node address is invariant across links as long as the node resides within a given site. Since the node address is used for transport connections, the latter do not break while nodes move around within a site. That is, intra-site node mobility is inherently provided. Locating a given node (reachability) is done through a normal link-state routing protocol like OSPFv3 or IS-IS for IPv6. No extra locators are necessary in SID6.

When a given node is a router, node mobility essentially means (sub-)network mobility. A whole subnet, along with the router and attached hosts, can move around within a site without losing reachability and transport connections. Instantaneous event-driven link-state updates will keep tight track of the moving subnet and the associated nodes.

A following consequence is that no Mobile IP protocol like MIPv6 [22] is necessary for intra-site mobile nodes. A MIPv6 client would be enabled only when a node visits a foreign site, and MIPv6 Home Agent (HA) needs to be installed only on AS border routers, not on every intra-site router. This simplification may stand for substantial resource saving in providing intra-domain mobility.

C. Faster Intra-Domain Mobility

Now a valid question might be whether intra-domain mobility provided by link-state routing protocols should be faster or slower than that provided by MIPv6-installed intra-site routers. First of all, movement detection by a mobile node should be the same for both cases; any of link-layer indication, Default Router (DR) not reachable, or a new prefix heard from RA, etc.; see Section 11.5.1 of MIPv6 [22]. Differences, if any, should be with the actions taken thereafter. Typical actions by a mobile node after movement detection, in accordance with MIPv6, should be:

1. Send RS (if no RA heard)
2. Receive RA to acquire prefix
3. Select DR
4. Create addresses including care-of-address
5. DAD for all unicast addresses
6. Register care-of-address with HA

Since the prefix acquired in Step 2 should be the same as the one already installed on the SID6 mobile node, Step 4 is to be skipped in SID6. Step 5 is not necessary, either, since uniqueness of the node ID(s) has already been guaranteed by previous site-wide DAD in accordance with the new DAD procedure introduced in Sec. III-C. Saving

DAD could be substantial since it would involve a number of message exchanges appended by possible retransmissions.

As for the last step, registering with HA may consume several Binding message exchanges. In the case of SID6, the mobile node would multicast an unsolicited NA to inform all nodes (including routers) on the newly visited link of its emergence. This would then be immediately followed by DR flooding an event-driven area-scoped link-state updates to inform all other intra-domain routers of the arrival of the visiting mobile node. Time lapses caused by the two schemes could be considered approximately equal.

As a result, time saving in SID6 should be what address creation and DAD would consume. Thus, intra-domain mobility provided by SID6 should be faster than MIPv6 by as much. This faster mobility would be a notable advantage in those Internet-of-Things applications where nodes would experience frequent changes in subnet attachment.

D. Seamless Multihoming

If a host is multi-homed on different links within a single-homed site, the node would be associated with only one node address since the prefixes would be the same for all different links. The node can be reached through any of these different links. With the usual IPv6 or some LIS protocols, each interface of the node would be given a distinct locator so that the peer node should choose between multiple locators to reach the same node, which task could be either arbitrary or complicated. With SID6, however, the node is associated with a single node address so that there'd be no confusion or extra work burden on the part of the peer node.

If a host is multi-homed on different sites, the node would possess multiple node addresses each derived from different global routing prefixes assigned by different upstream ISPs. Each of such node addresses is used to reach the node via the corresponding upstream ISP network. If a subnet is multi-homed on different sites, only the nodes within the very subnet would be given multiple node addresses each derived from prefixes assigned by different upstream ISPs. Nodes in other subnets would not be affected. If a site is multi-homed on different upstream ISPs, all nodes, either hosts or routers, would be given multiple node addresses derived from prefixes assigned by different upstream ISPs.

E. Legacy Renumbering

Renumbering can be done seamlessly as usual. The site would first be multi-homed on the old as well as the new ISP. Once all nodes are successfully renumbered and corresponding DNS records are updated, the old addresses would be removed and the site would be single-homed on the new ISP.

F. Legacy Inter-Domain Mobility

Inter-domain mobility would be done through MIPv6 as usual. HAs need be installed only on AS border routers.

G. Prefix Aggregation and Scalability

Prefix aggregation in DFZ is done as usual. That is, routing scalability of SID6 is as good as the legacy IPv6 networking.

H. Incremental Deployability

SID6 can be deployed incrementally. A site can adopt SID6, yet the external behavior of the site remains the same as a legacy IPv6 site.

I. Incentive for Deployment

The obvious incentive to deploy SID6 should be that transport connection resilience can be provided with no extra infrastructure like mapping servers found in most LIS protocols [5-7], resulting in significant resource saving. In addition, intra-domain mobility, and that faster, can be provided inherently by any intra-domain link-state protocols, with no hassle of installing MIPv6 functionality on every router in a site. Considering that a site can be arbitrarily large, this can be a considerable additional resource saving in terms of the network operation.

J. Security Considerations

SID6 should be as secure or insecure as the legacy IPv6 networking. As for privacy, there are proposals to hide node locality within a site [23-25]. Randomizing interface IDs works fine with SID6 since randomizing takes place only at node (re-)initialization once or not frequently enough [23].

Interface ID hashing is a function of not only routing prefix but also subnet ID [24, 25]; when a node moves to a foreign link, a new interface ID would be generated to hide the locality of the node from other hosts. In SID6, the hashed interface ID (thus node ID) would not change at such an intra-site move, and hence its locality would be exposed. However, this exposure is only to routers which keep locality information of nodes in their routing tables opaque to hosts. Hosts have no clue on which link other nodes reside or have moved to, except for on-link nodes in Neighbor Cache. Hosts would simply rely on DRs for packet deliveries to off-link nodes. Therefore, the privacy offered by [24, 25] would be scarcely affected.

VI. CONCLUSIONS

A network architecture based on local and recursive addressing is introduced. The Internet is seen as a collection of sites, each being itself a collection of nodes. Addresses local to a given sites name nodes whereas global addresses name sites. Mobility, of both hosts and subnets, should be fast because it is provided directly by routers as one of their inherent features. Frozen site- as well as node-addresses guarantee seamless site migration and multi-homing with no need for renumbering. Address depletion is not an issue anymore and the Internet governance reduces to a minimal necessity. The proposed network model can repeat itself outwards and inwards, enabling its applicability to inter-plenary Internet as well as to body area networks.

As a specific implementation example of NARA, the new IPv6 networking paradigm called SID6 is introduced, wherein the IPv6 subnet ID is deprecated, that is, set to zero. With such deprecation, interface IDs are site-local in SID6 in contrast to the legacy IPv6 networking wherein they are link-local. While the interface ID is used as the SID6 node ID for a node with a single interface, the interface ID of the minimum value is used as the node ID for a node with multiple interfaces.

With SID6, the task of simultaneous identification and location of a node, wrestled with by other LIS solutions through separate (ID and locator) number spaces, is accomplished without introducing a number space extra to that already available for node addresses. Furthermore, the job is done in two tiers; intra-site and inter-site:

- Within a site (intra-domain), node identification is provided through node IDs (or equivalently node addresses) while location is through an intra-domain link-state routing protocol.

- Across sites (inter-domain), identification is provided through (global) node addresses while location is by the global routing prefix.

With SID6, there's no need for deployment and management of the mapping servers (IDs versus locators), which should be a substantial resource saving over usual LIS solutions.

An additional advantage of SID6 is that intra-domain mobility is provided inherently by a link-state protocol, and that faster and more efficiently than with MIPv6. Moreover, HA need be installed only on site border routers, not on every intra-site router, thus resulting in another notable resource saving.

REFERENCES

[1] D. Meyer, L. Zhang, and K. Fall, "Report from the IAB Workshop on routing and addressing," The Internet Engineering Task Force, RFC 4984, 2007.

[2] A. Hinchley, "Issues in the Interconnection of Datagram Networks," IEN-1, Jul. 1977.

[3] J. Shoch, "Inter-network Naming, Addressing, and Routing," IEN-19, Jan. 1978.

[4] J. H. Saltzer, "On the naming and Binding of Network Destinations," The Internet Engineering Task Force, RFC 1498, 1993.

[5] R. Moskowitz and P. Nikander, "Host Identity Protocol (HIP) Architecture," The Internet Engineering Task Force, RFC 4423, May 2006.

[6] R. J. Atkinson, S. N. Bhatti, and U. St. Andrews, "Identifier locator network protocol (ILNP) architectural description," The Internet Engineering Task Force, RFC 6740, Nov. 2012.

[7] D. Farinacci, V. Fuller, D. Meyer, and D. Lewis, "The locator/ID separation protocol (LISP)," The Internet Engineering Task Force, RFC 6830, 2013.

[8] J. D. Day, Patterns in Network Architecture: A Return to Fundamentals, Boston, MA: Prentice Hall, 2008.

[9] P. Frejborg, "Hierarchical IPv4 Framework," RFC 6306, Jul. 2011.

[10] R. Hinden and S. Deering, "IP version 6 addressing architecture," The Internet Engineering Task Force, RFC 4291, 2006.

[11] R. Hinden, S. Deering, and E. Nordmark, "IPv6 global unicast address format,"

The Internet Engineering Task Force, RFC 3587, 2003.

[12] IAB/IESG, "IAB/IESG Recommendations on IPv6 address allocations to sites," The Internet Engineering Task Force, RFC 3177, 2001.

[13] A. Conta, S. Deering, and M. Gupta, "Internet control message protocol (ICMPv6) for the internet protocol version 6(ipv6) specification," The Internet Engineering Task Force, RFC 4443, 2006.

[14] T. Narten, E. Nordmark, W. Simpson, and H. Soliman, "Neighbor discovery for IP version 6 (IPv6)," The Internet Engineering Task Force, RFC 4861, 2007.

[15] H. Singh, W. Beebee, and E. Nordmark, "IPv6 subnet model: the relationship between links and subnet prefixes," The Internet Engineering Task Force, RFC 5942, 2010.

[16] S. Thomson, T. Narten, and T. Jinmei, "IPv6 stateless address autoconfiguration," The Internet Engineering Task Force, RFC 4862, 2007.

[17] R. Coltun, D. Ferguson, J. Moy, and A. Lindem, "OSPF for IPv6," The Internet Engineering Task Force, RFC 5340, 2008.

[18] C. Hopps, "Routing IPv6 with IS-IS," The Internet Engineering Task Force, RFC 5308, 2008.

[19] R. Callon, "Use of OSI IS-IS for routing in TCP/IP and dual environments," The Internet Engineering Task Force, RFC 1195, 1990.

[20] R. Droms, J. Bound, B. Volz, T. Lemon, C. Perkins, and M. Carney, "Dynamic host configuration protocol for IPv6 (DHCPv6)," The Internet Engineering Task Force, RFC 3315, 2003.

[21] D. Thaler, R. Draves, A. Matsumoto, and T. Chown, "Default address selection for internet protocol version 6 (IPv6)," The Internet Engineering Task Force, RFC 6724, 2012.

[22] D. Johnson, C. Perkins, and J. Arkko, "Mobility support in IPv6," The Internet Engineering Task Force, RFC 6275, 2011.

[23] T. Narten, R. Draves, and S. Krishnan, "Privacy extensions for stateless address autoconfiguration in IPv6," The Internet Engineering Task Force, RFC 4941, 2007.

[24] F. Gont, A. Cooper, D. Thaler, and W. Liu, "Recommendation on stable IPv6 interface identifiers," The Internet Engineering Task Force, RFC 8064, 2017.

[25] F. Gont, "A method for generating semantically opaque interface identifiers with IPv6 stateless address autoconfiguration (SLAAC)," The Internet Engineering Task Force, RFC 7217, 2014.

[26] Y. H. Kim, D. Y. Kim, and J. W. Park, "IPv6 Networking with a Deprecated Subnet ID," JCSE, vol. 11, no. 2, pp. 49-57, Jun. 2017.

[27] Y. H. Kim and D. Y. Kim, "NARA: Network Architecture with Recursive Addressing," Telecommunications Review, vol. 25, no. 2, pp. 261-273, 2015.

Printed by Books on Demand GmbH, Norderstedt / Germany